BLUE
WINDOW

BLUE WINDOW

Poems by
Deborah Gordon Cooper

CLOVER
VALLEY
PRESS

Clover Valley Press, LLC
Duluth, Minnesota

Clover Valley Press, LLC
6286 Homestead Rd.
Duluth, MN 55804-9621
USA

Cover design and original art by Stacie Renné, i.e. design

Printed in the United States of America on acid-free paper.

Library of Congress Control Number: 2017944061

ISBN: 978-0-9973643-2-3

Acknowledgments

A number of the poems in the Nightlife section were first published in *Wide Awake, Every Week* (Big Little Bay LLC, 2015).

I owe an enormous debt of gratitude to the Cill Rialaig Artists Retreat in County Kerry, Ireland, for the gift of the residency, the opportunity to write and dream in such a hauntingly beautiful landscape.

My thanks to my teaching partner, Gary Boelhower, and all of the poets at the St. Louis County Jail.

A heart full of thanks also to my faithful Writing Group. And to Charlene Brown, my publisher and my friend, for consistently believing in me.

For my children,
Amy, Dylan, and Madeline,
whose loving kindness sustains me.

For my grandchildren,
Cooper, Ivy, Graham, and Owen,
each one a shining light.

For Joel, my truest home.

Contents

III. Deliverance

IV. Kismet

The day after
the night I dreamed

that, folding laundry,
my hands kept catching fire

I began writing poems.

I. Nightlife

It Begins

It begins

ten thousand miles away,
across a turbulence of sea

the whispered words
of a prayer,
a breath,
a benediction

carried on the shoulders
of the waves

beneath the sun's watch
and the moon's

carried on the shoulders
of the waves

the waves that taper to a river;
the river tapers to a stream

a stream that tumbles
over stones
to reach the nest

the heron's nest, tucked
like a secret
in the reeds

a breath that sleeps
in the fragile beat
in the dark of the egg

till it is lifted
on white wings

white wings, reflected
in your eyes. ¬

I WANTED TO TELL YOU

I wanted to tell you
the way the white heron,
rising,
lifted a part of me away

and the missing
in the part of me
that stayed,
what is the name for that?

I want the right phrase
for this last orange ribbon
of light

trembling now
upon the lake's pale skin.

What do we call
this hue
of longing?

I want a way to describe
looking out at the glittered sky

through my mother's eyes,
nine years beyond her death

how it is we know
we are inhabited . . .

Deborah Gordon Cooper

the moon,
slowly lowering
the veil. ¬

BLUE MOON

Though she cannot see it
from the bed

the blue moon coaxes her
from sleep

the way a mother
wakes a child

the slight, warm weight
of a hand

a voice, lilting and falling
in a soft refrain.

She lifts the sheet,
eases her way

to the seat
beneath the window

watches the moon's
subtle descent

the movement echoing
inside her

extinguished finally by
the windswept sea.

He sighs and breathes,
vaguely aware

on the periphery
of sleep

the vacant space
beside him in the bed

gradually growing cold. ¬

SECRETS THE CURTAINS KEEP

The secrets
in the woman's hands

drawing the curtains closed
as darkness falls, a sigh,
cordial *good nights*

above the current
of the words
unspoken.

The secrets
in the woman's dreams

unfolding in the air
above the bed

the intermittent image
of a man

not the one
sleeping dreamlessly
beside her.

The secrets
in the woman's hands

parting the curtains
for the dawn

the lingering
trill of longing
in her fingers. ﹁

NIGHTLIFE

Awake again
at 3 a.m.

jumble of thoughts,
the way socks tumble
in a dryer

moving in the dark,
window to window

through these rooms
I know by heart

the tick and creak
and whispers
of the house . . .

ah, there,
hung in the branches
of the oak tree

that we planted
when he died

the soft, lopsided lantern
of the moon.

Across the street
and down the block

across the city,
in a farmhouse
miles away

in other rooms,
at other windows

other women
are awake

lifted by worry, lifted by
the infant's stirring
or the child's urgent cry

lifted by memory,
premonition

or by yearning

by the persuasion
of the moon. ⁓

I WANT A LANGUAGE

I want a language for
the murmuring of rain
in the night

speaking a promise
of forgiveness

the way we ease
into the same dream,
a dream we won't remember

though it is there,
in the hollow of the throat.

I want the word
that saves
your heartbeat
in my ear

the way,
as a child,
I saved the sea
in shells.

I want the word
that saves
your heartbeat
in my ear

long after
I raise my head
from your chest
and leave you. ⌐

PEONIES AND RAIN

She sees the radiant peonies
bow their great heads in prayer

in praise, in supplication,
in the early morning rain.

In the not-quite-light,
she slips outside
to join their silent congregation.

Sprinkling of holy water
brings her to her knees,
in praise, in supplication.

She prays with peonies.

Over toast, he notices
her hair is soaked.

He must have slept
right through her shower.

But then he notices
her nightdress
is drenched too.

And when she goes
to fill her teacup,
he can see her knees
are caked with mud

which makes him wonder,
though he doesn't ask. ⌐

Unbidden

In the dark,
far away
across the hills

as if a single pulse of light
had graced the dark side
of the moon

a trace of memory
unbidden
wakes his hidden heart

a trace of memory,
then taken by the wind

the wind that passes
like a shiver
through the wilderness of pine

a whisper tossed
from crown to crown

and softens finally
with the dawn's light
to this breeze

ruffling the leaves
of the oak tree
in the yard

Deborah Gordon Cooper

the yellow nightgown
swaying on the line

a trace of memory, released
in the plaintive song
of a chickadee

caught in the intricate curl
of your ear. ⁃

Waiting on the Light

Awake at five,
the sunrise still
two hours away

I feel my way
toward the window

my outstretched fingers
graze the wall

trace the tall back
of the old couch.

A threadbare shawl
around my shoulders,
like a loved one's arms.

I am still half-tangled
in a dream,
its gauzy net
caught on my ankle.

I am waiting
on the light.

Through the glass
I watch the shadows
take their shapes

Deborah Gordon Cooper

a neighbor's gate,
the naked maples.

My own body
gathers me back in.
Asleep, I filled the house.

When the first bird lifts
her crystal song
into the winter air

splits the seam
between the world
and sky

I'll lay the fire
and put the kettle on.

Once I thought
with every dawn
all things are possible.

My thoughts
are smaller now.

I hold them
in my hands. ¬

LIKE STARS

Like stars,
long after their deaths

their light still finds me. ¬

Deborah Gordon Cooper

SHAWL OF STARLIGHT

blue, blue windows
behind the stars
~Neil Young

Last night, the stars
outside my undraped window
wakened me.

Held within their gaze,
I couldn't close my eyes,
lose hold of the connection.

When at last I turned,
I felt the constellations
fall across my shoulders

a Brahms Sonata
on a piano
in some distant room. ¬

MY PIANO

for Drew

My piano has been silent
for years,
since the dying began.

The weight of even
the most gentle notes,
unbearable.

Friends tell me
He would want you to play.

But all I know
with certainty
is this:
He didn't want to die.

I sit by my piano and knit,
two mute companions
in a room.

Each of us with songs inside,
longing to be sung. ⌐

Deborah Gordon Cooper

By Grace

Today,
whether by alchemy
or grace

the music,
so long dormant,
wakes in me

and what's been frozen
since the moment
of his death

lifts in my chest . . .

each note unfolding
in my hands
upon the piano keys.

Today,
whether by grace
or synchronicity

the amaryllis
in the winter window
blooms. ⌐

WHAT SEWS YOU TO ME, THEN?

This sheet of music,
written by your hand

played by my hands
upon the keys

the binding stitches
of these notes

the silver needle
of this melody. ¬

WHAT SHE LEAVES US

All that time
we had been making
something invisible
at her direction

the way a spider finds
inside herself
the makings of a home
in every circumstance

a way across what looks
like only emptiness
or devastation
or the dark.

All that time
as her body dimmed,
and as her spirit
caught a light
we could not see
without her

we moved and stumbled
at her cue,
stepping in and holding,
stepping back again,
out of her way.

All that time
she let us help her
weave this net,
less, now we see

to guard the safety
of her crossing
than to hold us
to each other
afterwards

after her hand
had slipped entirely
from our grasp. ¬

I'm Sorry I Cannot Refill The Feeder

I'm sorry I cannot refill the feeder

because of the web suspended
in between it and a neighboring branch

its silken strands illumined
in the early light.

How intricate
and how precarious our lives.

To appease the chattered pleading
of the chickadees

I scatter seed along the railing
of the deck.

I worry when the winds rise. ¬

IMPERMANENCE
for Judi

That whole afternoon
in Nashville of all places
we watch Tibetan monks
create a sand mandala,
grain by richly colored grain.

We are entranced.
Now and then our hands meet
or our eyes.
We know that we are caught
in something holy.
They work for seven days
and nights.

We return to see it finished,
breathless,
stunning in its intricate detail,
each nook and hue and border
meaning something else.

When the monks begin to chant
it is a song like frogs and cellos
and night wind,
a sound that moves right through
the hollow reeds
our bodies have become.

Then they wreck it,
stir it up, undone.
Impermanence.

The round monk
with the kindest eyes
hands me a tiny bag of sand.
Release it into moving water
for the healing of the world.
He bows away.

I am not good at this.
I spill a bit of it at Easter
into Gooseberry,
and let some go in August
up at Grand Marais,
the waves applauding at my feet.

But I hold back
and now a year has galloped past
and I still hoard
this tablespoon of sand.
I cannot open up my hands
completely.

I am unshakably attached,
to limbs and rocks
and to the first shy eyes
of flowers in the spring,
to people's voices
and their hands.

To the particular loveliness
of each small thing . . .
this tiny bowl of colored sand,
this cobalt mug,
this afghan Nana knit,
Joel's body in this bed. ¬

II. Blue Window

First Night in Cill Rialaig
for Lynn Marie

You are home

swept up in the first
dark wings of grief

and I am far away.

I cannot sleep.
I cannot reach you.

I kneel on the bed
to see out through
the tiny window

set high in the stone wall.

I kneel on the bed,
a child's posture,
while the hours crawl by.

No moon in the sky,
no stars . . .

the heavy curtains
of the clouds
closed.

At last,
a muted light,
scant hope of dawn.

Deborah Gordon Cooper

Mist, like sorrow,
shrouds the islands
in the bay.

The skin of the sea
begins to shiver
in the rain.

Three strands
of birdsong
tremble in the air

a supplication,
braiding
and unbraiding.

Somewhere
in the fog
that drapes the hills

a lamb is bleating
for its mother. ¬

TODAY, A CONSOLATION

Sheep on the cliffs,
the cattle in the byre

a spill of yellow flowers
paints the hills.

Ten thousand stories,
sleeping in these stones

ten thousand stories, wakened
in ten thousand dreams.

Lost voices, lifted
in the waves,
the wind,
the keening gulls

a penny whistle
and a fiddle
and a drum.

Some days,
a torment takes the seas.

Last night,
a haunting song,
a throng of longing.

Today,
a consolation
in these waves

Deborah Gordon Cooper

soothing hands
upon the furrowed
brow of shore.

Here, a thousand
kindnesses
of green

a thousand variations
on the theme
of sky. ¬

BLUE WINDOW

In the wee hours,
I dream another woman's dreams

the dream of the boat;
the dream of the garden,
sweet peas and cabbages.

Wake with her story
in my mouth

potatoes, rotting
in the ground . . .

the news,
passed house to house

a whole family,
fallen on the mountainside

clung together,
a tangle of limbs

one after another,
gone.

The man beside her,
shuddering the bed
with sobs

shaking off the comfort
in her hand.

She turns away,
makes of her bones
a wall to shelter him.

When one child
or another

cries with hunger
in its sleep,
she sings the lullaby

filling the cottage,
every cranny,
with the sound of it.

The last child born,
she would not let go

held to her breast
the whole night long,
and not a drop of milk.

The last child born,
gone to stone in her arms

unnamed and unredeemed.

Certain sleepless nights,
through the blue window

set high in the stones
above the bed

she watches the sky
for a sign,
for a glimmer.

She prays the rosary,
the beating stars,
her beads . . .

wishes she still believed
the rosary
might save them. ⌐

Deborah Gordon Cooper

THE CHESTNUT HARE

Climbing the steep path
to Bolus Head

through slanting fields
of sheep

a chestnut hare
lopes gracefully
toward me.

Before me now,
he stands
tall

just above me
on the sharp incline

so that we're almost
eye to eye

mine, timid
and a startled blue.

His eyes are amber
and untroubled

and the sheep
on the hills
bow their heads

and the birds
and the distant bells
go silent.

His golden eyes
open windows
to a hidden world

and there *you* are
behind them,
looking out at me

and the wind
holds its breath

and the clouds
crossing the sky
pause

and the roiling sea
rests

the sea rests. ⌐

Deborah Gordon Cooper

EARLY MORNING EAVESDROPPING

Each sheep has its own unique voice,
actually saying baa with a distinct b.

They don't sound like real sheep at all,
but like people pretending to be sheep.

Sometimes they bleat in harmony,
basses, tenors, altos, and sopranos.
One of the altos is consistently off key.

After a week or so of attentive listening,
I can begin to decipher their moods . . .

the babies, of course,
calling for their mothers,
who quite often feign deafness

the squeal-of-delight bleat
when they spot their own mums

the bored bleat

the testy bleat

the arrogant bleat

the pleading bleat

the friendly Irish *hi ya* and *cheerio* bleats
when you pass by the field

a ring of pride in this greeting
when you meet on the path

the sheep
having gotten
free of the fence

a sheep's fondest dream.

Perhaps it is ours too.

Later, Tadhg and Michael
chat outside my window

the rise and fall
of ancient Irish

like a melody,
a morning canticle

the sun
unraveling
the fog. ⌐

CARTOGRAPHIES

And then they come
to that portion
of the map

that folded corner
where the names
of things

the hamlet
and the mountain,
the ravine

are not the same
for every wanderer.

Here, just the thought
of azure

the slightest notion
of a wooden boat,
a scarlet sail

and, for one traveler,
it's the whisper
of the river

for one,
the wild irises
embellishing the banks

while for another,
it's the breeze
that thrills the sail.

Beyond the bend,
the suggestion
of a yew tree

in what might be
the crumbled ruins
of an abbey.

For him,
it is deciphering
the structure
in the stones.

For her,
it is the vespers
and the hymns

lingering
in the limbs
of the ancient tree.

To the south,
the shadowed shapes
that might be horses
in a field.

He names the breeds,
listing their origins
and strengths.

She sees the gate
swing free

dune grass beyond,
white splay of sand

and open sea. ⌐

LAST NIGHT IN CILL RIALAIG, FULL MOON

The moon, behind
the sheerest sails
of cloud

casts subtle shadows
on these hills

an open gate,
a standing stone,
a bending hawthorn tree

while casting
pools of moonlight
on the darkened sea.

She has kept her watch
across the ages

over what's been lost,
and what's been saved

over all passages
and partings.

The map of memory
is written in her face. ⌐

While We Were Away

While we were away

the daffodils
have come

and shone

and gone
without us.

But the blossoms
on the lilac boughs
have been sketched in,
a rudimentary design.

Thinking of Ellie
in her yard
across the bay
(a famous measurer of blooms)

I count the buds
that crown the peonies.

Thinking of Candace
on the Point

the way she tromps
through April snow

to find the pussy willows,
hidden in the trees

I dream of trilliums,
beneath the lattice
of new-green.

I dream of trilliums,
and count the promises
of peonies. ﹁

Deborah Gordon Cooper

AT LAST

At last
in increments
too gradual to measure

as if the sun
has had the slightest
shift of heart

the light slips back.

The songs
collected in our throats

press
for an opening. ¬

MORNING, EARLY APRIL, CORNUCOPIA
EMAIL FROM ELLIE IN DULUTH

She tells me
she is sitting,
sipping coffee

in a lawn chair
on the deck

planning to plant pansies
in the window box
sometime this afternoon.

Looking out
across the mounds of snow

across the miles of ice
still holding the lake captive,
I imagine her.

In my mind
she is wearing a fur coat
that had belonged to her mother

and a pansy-purple scarf.

And I think that she is crazy.
And I think she is tenacious.

And I think she is a woman
of the utmost faith

though I know
this is a claim
she would deny. ⌐

MY DAUGHTER SENDS ME
PHOTOGRAPHS FROM MAUI

Lush flowers
in outlandish pinks
and scarlets.

I comb,
with careful,
frigid fingers

the scrap of garden
on the south side
of the house

brushing off snow,
coaxing the crocuses.

A throng of birds sweeps in,
moving as one wide wing

waking the naked branches
of the maple trees,
a carnival of song

each note,
a secret, curled
into a chrysalis

an origami flower,
folded in a bud. ¬

Light's Gravity

Bulbs crack
in the black earth.

A tight seed splits,
releasing coiled green.

First tiny tree buds,
bursting at the seams.

Light's gravity . . .
the homeward pull begins.

Swallows and starlings,
maps hidden in their wings.

And the thrush blows its song
on the bones of the dead

and the bones of the dead
break into blossoms. ⌐

RAVENS AND BLOSSOMS IN MORNING LIGHT:
INTERPRETATIONS

A raven lands,
shadow first, upon
the grass

frets and struts
beneath gnarled branches
of an apple tree

a fall of blossoms,
loosened by
the morning breeze

white petals,
blue-black feathers,
dappled light

the raven, nattering
and keening.

A woman, watering
the pansies,
stops to watch.

She understands this
as a promise
from her husband

from her husband,
gone one year.

Deborah Gordon Cooper

Her soft hand flutters
at her chest.

The vicar, on a porch
across the street,
can only read this
as an omen

a foreboding
of a darkness
soon to come.

He feels the first throes
of an undertow.

A young girl
with a cloud
of wind-tossed hair

gazes, waving
from a window

still half tangled
in the sheets

and in the remnants
of a dream
of flight.

A boy on a bike
tosses the papers

papers rolled up
tight as clubs

fleeing the harsh words
that broke the night
again.

He hurls a paper
at the target
of a door.

A raucous call,
a leap . . .
a shadow
scales the apple tree

takes to the sky. ¬

DETOURS

A man, at a stoplight-turned-green,
is lost in memories,
a thousand miles away.
A car behind him honks,
rattling him back.

A preacher rambles on
in black and white.

A woman in a pew
takes in instead
the way the flowers
on the altar
open to the light.

A boy falls asleep
between the pages
of a book,
lands in the story
and the plot twists.

A girl crossing a field
is caught
by a butterfly,
arrives home late for supper.

Ninety-four and disappearing
by degrees,
a woman sees a flock of starlings
sweep the sky.

With just the effort of a wish
she lifts to join them. ¬

III. Deliverance

CENTRAL HILLSIDE:
MAY MORNING

Minnie hears the thud of the mail
on the entry floor
and bends to pick it up.
Her back complains.

Tucked in the ads
and the bills
is a card from her son,
a few days late
but still.

It is a simple one,
no frills,
just *happy mother's day*
his name scrawled at the bottom.

She remembers the way
when Ollie's rage erupted,
fists and dishes in the air,
she'd slink off to her room
with a whimper,
lock the door

leaving Dennis
in the center
of the storm.

She adds a splash
of brandy
to her tea.

Across the street
Bea adds fresh water
to the roses
that her daughter sent.

She keeps her voice
light and cheery
on the phone.

She can handle this alone.
She is the strong one.

Even Emil doesn't know
what the doctor told her,
his eyes glued to the chart.

MAY EVENING

Ray's working late again.
Ruth makes herself a sandwich,
takes it out onto the porch,
first trace of blossoms
in the air.

She sees the older couple
down the block
filling up their window boxes
with a summer's-worth of blooms.

The old man stops,
walks over to his wife,
puts his arm around her shoulder.

Watching this,
Ruth tries to picture
her own life at seventy . . .

and sees herself alone,
on a porch, a sandwich
in her hand.

At that same moment,
Emil whispers in Bea's ear
I wish that we could go back
thirty years.
She wonders if he knows
what's coming after all.

Early Morning, Late July

Her slippers whispering
across the kitchen floor
repeat the morning's choreography,
counter to sink to canister
and back,
and it is in that movement
traced a thousand times before

that Ruth decides she'll leave him
once the summer's passed
without a warning.

Everything that's held them
to each other
has already frayed.

Perhaps she'll leave a note
I've gone away
and she imagines just the way
he'll turn it over in his hand,
but then he'll open the refrigerator door
as if she might have left
a casserole.

Across the plots of yards
outside the yellow house,
red blossoms at the windows,
a gray cat dozes on the rug.

Inside, a mug of coffee
in his hand,
Emil climbs the stairs to wake her,
rests his lips against
the silvery wisps of hair
and breathes her name.
In an hour he'll take her in
for chemo.

And while they run the potion
through her veins
he'll skip the coffee
and the hardware store
to sit within the church's stony silence,
to try to purchase
with his promises
at least the time until
the leaves have turned.
The fall has always been
her favorite season.

Up and down the street
a slight boy on a red bike
pitches the papers.

Minnie watches from her window
and goes soft, thinking of
her own son
seven states away.

This boy is fast.
Last night the yelling yanked him
out of sleep again
and now he must be accurate,
make no mistakes,
complete his route
in record time.

Some nights the wind is kind.
Ribbons of lullabies
in languages he cannot understand
spill through the screens.

Some nights
he counts the headlights
as they race across the wall,
waits for the birds
to call the sun up.

THANKSGIVING

Inside the door
that doesn't fit its frame
and lets in tentacles of cold,
Minnie chops celery
for stuffing
and wonders why
she bought a turkey
after all.

Her son will not be coming,
a new baby
and she hasn't seen the last one.
Once he sent a picture
in a card.
She thought the girl
might look like her, though
no one's ever said as much.

Three times she stops,
wiping her hands
upon her apron,
dials the phone
and lets it ring.

She knows that Emil's home
across the street.
She sees the lights go on and off
behind the windows
of the yellow house.
And though she doesn't want to be alone,
she's still uncertain what she'll say.
She never made it to the funeral.

Beneath the lamp
that was a wedding gift
so long ago,
Emil holds the paper
without taking in the words,
startles at the phone
each time it rings
as if forgetting how to stop it.

Later, in the dissipating light,
Minnie fills a plate
and takes it over.
When he won't come to the door
she leaves it waiting
on the stoop,

Deborah Gordon Cooper

pleasing the cat, who's only fed
haphazardly these days.

Two boys in winter jackets
on their bicycles
come clattering down the street.

When the small one waves
she is so grateful
that she almost
starts to cry.

Down the street
a couple eats their turkey
by the light of the TV,
something Ruth swore
she'd never do.
It hardly matters now.

But when Ray leans toward her,
reaches out so that his fingers
trace her cheek,
something asleep
inside her stirs.

Such a tiny gesture
and it changes
the direction
of the wind.

Perhaps she'll stay.

FEBRUARY

Two boys are playing hockey
in the street.
Sweeping snow from the porch,
Ruth guesses at their ages.

If the baby had lived
he would've been nine
next week.

He is the silence
in between them.
They never tried again.

Surprising herself, she wonders
if it's too late now.

Emil's daughter Betsy
blusters in,
a box of chocolates in her hand

discovers some new horror
with each stride

her mother's jacket
hanging on the coat rack
Dad, it's almost been five months!

A stain of splattered coffee
on his shirt

Deborah Gordon Cooper

Go change now, and I'll soak it.

A stack of dirty dishes in the sink,
puddle of cat pee on the floor.
That cat needs to be put down, Dad.
It should have been done long ago.

Once she leaves
he takes the heart-shaped
box of chocolates
across the street
and knocks on Minnie's door. ˗

DARK CLOUDS THIS MORNING

Dark clouds this morning,
casting shadows on the waves.

And still, the birds sing . . .
one of sorrow, two of grace. ⌐

Deborah Gordon Cooper

Ever After

Falling rain soaks
the golden maples,
but the leaves hold on.

Sitting at the table
in the kitchen

you write a poem
about your mother's death

the thread of longing
that never lets go

though it might loosen
here and there

might go unnoticed
for days at a time

tightens
as you write these lines,
tea going cold.

Now, in a space
between words

slipping in between
the dripping leaves

a trace of sunlight
weaves its way

reaching for your hand
upon the table. ¬

FALL OF LOSSES

For one brief
blessed moment

in that state before
complete awakening

he dreams
or he believes
that he is young again

that Beatrice sleeps beside him,
a fleeting, sweet amnesia

then, the weary
aching in his limbs.

He lumbers up,
makes instant coffee

drains the cup,
puts on his battered cap.

While he slept
fall fell
without a sound

tumbled, rust
and brown
across the yard

across the memory
of her garden.

He works and rests
in measured time.

Stopping, he fumbles
for his gloves

unpocketing the rosary

his gnarled fingers
drop the beads.

He sweeps them up
among the leaves

putting his life in order. ¬

Deborah Gordon Cooper

Talking to Strangers

An old man
in a coffee shop
in Nipigon

tells me stories
of his childhood

the year his family lived
inside a chicken coop

the smell his mother
couldn't bleach away,
the way it lingered
in their clothes.

They ate oatmeal
twice a day,
bowing their heads
for grace

Bless us, O Lord,
and these Thy gifts

and once,
on Christmas morning,
gift of oranges
outside the door.

Three apiece

the small boy
still there,
in his eyes

and one for Mum. ¬

Deborah Gordon Cooper

PAS DE DUEX

Every week
Lee takes
his aging lover
to the Parkinson's
ballet class.

Lee bellies up
to the barre.
Stan shuffles over,
his own version
of glissade.

Demi-plié,
a trembling relevé.

So this is love. ¬

THE POETRY READING

At the poetry reading
in the gym
of the county jail

Billy,
who doesn't belong there

who looks to be about twelve years of age

Billy,
whose only crime
is being homeless

and disturbed,
afraid

flails his thin arms
and hands in the air

like a trapped bird

frantically rocking
in the flimsy chair.

A man walks in

the man
awaiting trial,
facing eighteen years.

Deborah Gordon Cooper

The man walks in,
chooses the chair
beside the boy

and, without moving,
in the silent way
a leaf unfolds

he grows a wide wing
of kindness.

He grows a wide wing
of kindness

as beside him,
Billy quiets
incrementally

drawn slightly in

his face,
in that brief interlude
of grace

reclaiming its true,
original beauty. ¬

THE WOMEN'S GROUP

Nikki, rocking slightly
in the chair

reads her poem
about the baby's death

holds her slender arm
across her chest

a safety belt
of bones
and skin

the baby's name,
a bracelet, tattooed
on her wrist, *Demetri*

her fist, in the
hollowed space

between her shoulder
and the beating
of her heart. ¬

DELIVERANCE

We bring pictures
to poetry class

paintings and photographs

a splay of color
to awaken
the monotony

dazzle the memory
from slumber.

That night, I dream . . .

A kind C.O.
wheels a tea cart
to the women's block

finds no one there.

I feign bewilderment,
though in my mind
I see

the wandering river

three white horses
in a field

a single candle,
glowing in a window.

I feign bewilderment,
though in my mind
I see

the bridge
above the canyon

Van Gogh's *Starry Night*

the raven
in the treetop

poised for flight. ⌐

Deborah Gordon Cooper

In Poetry Class at the Jail

Derek talks about the moon

the moon he can see
through the window of his cell

for seven lucky minutes
every night it's clear.

Then Justin talks about the moon
that rose above the barn

on the farm of his seventh foster family,
the way it soothed his loneliness.

Bart writes a poem about the memory
of moonlight upon snow

when he was only nine,
first time he ran away.

Josh recalls a winter
on the streets, fifteen

the coldest nights, spent
huddled in a dumpster.

We write in silence then.

When they're led back to their blocks
for lockdown, I head home.

A pale moon sails
the darkening canopy of sky

from wide horizon
to horizon. ¬

Deborah Gordon Cooper

Van Gogh's Starry Night

seen through the iron-barred
window of his asylum cell

A glimpse
of the moon, seen
through a high window

even a window
that you cannot reach

even the window
of a cell

lifts you
in that moment
from your darkness.

I wonder,
in the absence
of a window

if just the memory
of the moon
might be enough. ¬

REFUGEES

I imagine this moon
unraveling the city

the makeshift village,
cobbled on the shore

the trampled wilderness

the broken dreams
of children

the sound of hope
going out

in the throats
of the old ones

the way of all lost languages.

What is it
that cracks open
the tight kernel
of meanness

unknots the fists.

What is it
that soothes
the harsh edges
of stones

lodged in the heart.

What light is this
that seeks its way
into the world

without an edict
or an argument

through any crevice,
any fissure in the wall?

What slender key
unlocks the gate
and sends the guards away?

What makes a space in us
to harbor one another? ¬

HOPE MOVES UPON THE WATERS

It might be terror
that propels us.
It might be hunger
or despair.

But it is hope
that bears us.

Hope moves upon the waters.

And, though the threads unfurl
across the distances,
they do not break

the threads that bind us . . .
to our landscape,
to our language,
to a loved one's face.

Hope moves upon the waters

in the shape of a boat,
in the shape
of a makeshift raft

a lone figure in a river
on a moonless night.

Hope moves upon the waters. ¬

Deborah Gordon Cooper

COME TO THE WATER

Every network blares
the same bad news.

Come away,
clutching your troubles
in tight fists

to where the water
will unravel you

threading the same prayer
through all the ages

while the generations
come and go,
rising and folding.

Lay your open palms
upon the cedar tree

bowed over
with the memory
of frost, of fire

till the life of the tree
beats in your own blood.

The smallest child
standing by the water
knows

which stone to keep
and which one
to let go. ¬

IV. Kismet

KISMET

Fort William, Ontario 1942

Because my father missed
the last bus back

he met my mother
at the music store. ⌐

Deborah Gordon Cooper

THE PHOTOGRAPH

Looking frantically for something
I've misplaced,
an extra key, a bill, a poem,
I ransack drawers,
come upon a photograph of you
and flinch
as if I'd cut my hand.

There you are, whole,
at the bottom of the drawer.
Smiling in your lab coat
by the regiment of books, medical texts,
some of them written by you
and I remember your pride
when they came in the mail,
your careful unwrapping.
Passing them around the supper table,
we'd applaud.
You knew everything then.

I bend to the floor,
your face in my hands.
I had forgotten how handsome you were,
how lean and quick and eager
to explain the world,
the constellations
and the names of clouds and bones,
the mechanism of the heart.

There you stand
looking right out of your eyes.
You rarely come up to
those windows anymore.

Some days you sit in the same spot,
like a locked house.
My love keeps bouncing
off your walls,
trying to get in. ¬

LIKE POSTCARDS

for my father

You left long before
the day you died

your vacant body
beating on

your lungs
like bellows
in the rain.

Once they had stopped
it seemed
you floated back again.

Those first blurred weeks
I'd catch you
hovering around.

Your voice would wake me
in the night

some tiny magnet
in my heart
tilting to find you.

Later, I lost hold of you,
as if you'd moved beyond
my field of gravity.

I found you then in things
you'd left behind

inside the sleeves
of your gray sweater

in the pages of your books,
the blue squiggles of your hand
filling the margins.

Once I saw my name there
Deb might like this
and I did.

Then one day
I had to use a photograph
to figure out your face.

You still send
the occasional message

a blue-black feather
on your grave

a dragonfly that lights
upon my arm

like postcards
to a loved one
in the old country. ¬

HER HANDS

The last year, her hands
curled into knots

the hands that brought the music
to my childhood

Chopin floating up the stairway
while I fell asleep.

It was work at the end,
opening her hands

to wash them and massage
the lotion in

then fasten on the sheepskin-covered splints
to keep her fingernails from digging through
the pale, fragile skin of her palms.

Holding her hand meant wrapping yours
around a tight bundle of bones.

How is it then, that in
this photograph

taken the day she saw the baby
the first time

the hand she lays upon his head
is the soft, curved wing of a bird? ¬

Waking the Dead

for my mother

All these years,
I've kept your rosaries
safe

safe in the glass case
upon the shelf

draped over
the gray basalt
and shining beach glass

from the shores of the lake
you gave me as a child.

Today I lift the lid
on its fragile hinges
and choose one

the heavy one
carved out of
Connemara marble

sturdy enough
for your fumbling fingers
to hold on to
those last years

obey their clumsy
choreography.

As if they'd been waiting
for this moment
in my mouth

the prayers
I haven't spoken
since your death

flow from my lips
without the obstacle
of thought. ⌐

I Dream of Canada

Somewhere between
the border
and the edge
of Thunder Bay

I stop the car,
walk the path
up to a house
tucked in the bluffs

a house I've never seen before,
a house I recognize.
The door is open.

They are sitting
at the table
in the kitchen.

They are sitting
sipping tea,
as if they hadn't died at all.

My father's eyes
are wide awake.
My father's lights are on.

My father calls me
by my name.
My father knows me.

Deborah Gordon Cooper

My mother smiles,
rising from her chair

without a hoyer lift,
without a transfer belt,
without assist of one

my mother rises from her chair,
strides toward me,
takes me in.

I don't know
that I believe
in Heaven.

I only know
I'd rather be
in Canada. ⌐

CROSSING THE BORDER

I've come to Canada
in search of something
I've lost hold of

something essential,
slipped away.

Its absence
in the hollow
of my throat

the ghost beneath
the breastbone.

Here, traces
of a scent
caught in the breeze

awake a stirring
at the farthest reach
of memory.

The giant,
sleeping still,
as in my childhood.

The giant's dreams,
still carried by the waves

carried away
in all directions.

Standing high above the lake,
heart-stopping drop
of cliff

and far below,
primordial heartbeat
of the waves

a pulse that echoes
through my veins

sews me back
into my own skin.

In Canada
I sleep
in my childhood's posture

arms open,
wide as wings.

In Canada
I dream again
of trees

of ancient secrets,
lifted in the breeze

whispered
in the drumbeat
of the waves.

The leaves and the lake
speak with the same voice

the same wind,
stirring the same songs

through the trees
and through the waters

and in all our depths
and limbs

a breath that never ends
begins again,
begins. ¬

Deborah Gordon Cooper

THE LAKE

The Lake
is opening the dark
again.
She prays the sun up
every morning

slips it from
beneath her silver skirts,
holds fire
in her hands.

Her voice
repeats its mantra.
Her reaching fingers curl

murmuring
over the smooth stones
like a rosary.

At night
she lifts the moon
out of her pocket,
like a sacrament

falls
over and over
to her knees
upon the shore. ¬

I Only Know

I only know
if you are still enough
and wait

you'll hear the songs
the stones remember. ¬

Late Summer
Sleeping on the Porch

The full moon casts
a spell of shadows
on our sleep

draping patterns
of the trees
across the grass

igniting fireflies.

On the lake, a ship
made out of light

is floating
in slow motion
to the port.

A melancholy
loon duet
at 4 a.m.

and soon,
pink seeps
into the linen
of the sky.

I save these images

the moon, the fireflies,
the ship of lights,
the loons

the way, later today
we'll split and stack
the wood

to ease us
through the winter. ⌐

Deborah Gordon Cooper

THE WEIGHT OF MAPLE

I carry in wood
from the shed

the weight of maple
like a promise
in my arms

cut from the tree
we sacrificed
to build the shed

the shed, now
sheltering its bones

bones that,
even in this moment

burn and sing
their fragrant offerings
of warmth and light

to soothe
the falling darkness.

Wisps of memory
lift free

snowflakes and stars,
a breeze

first fragile leaves
unfolding

the weave of a nest,
tucked in the crook
of its limbs. ¬

Painting of the Farm
In Shades of Blue

It is the first thing
I lay eyes on

in the day's
first trace of light

the blue-gray farmhouse
where it all began

wind's sweep
of silvery snowdrifts
drape the yard

indigo shadows
of the cottonwoods

the winter twilight's
pure cerulean sky.

I glimpse the image
of my younger self

framed in
the nursery window

with a baby
in my arms.

Now, I'm in the window
of the parlor

looking out
across bare orchards
and white fields

my younger hand,
lifting the lace

looking out
across the distances
and decades

looking out
across calamity
and grace

looking out
across the tenderness
and longing

my own astonishment
reflected in my face. ¬

Deborah Gordon Cooper

DREAM OF THE OLD FARMHOUSE

The picket fence that friends built
as a wedding gift;
the sheets and diapers on the line.

Inside, the crooked floors;
cabbage roses on
the wallpaper, unraveling.

I stoke the fire in the woodstove,
haul the water from the well;
realize I need to feed the children,
lift the soup pot from the shelf.

But then, a door I'd never seen before.
I turn the knob . . .

a sky-blue room
with Irish lace
upon the window,
a piano in the corner
and a single wicker chair.

And I know
what the poem
on the open page of the book
beside the chair will be;
what the sheet music
on the piano will be.

And I know
when I lift the lace
of the curtain,
I will see the orchard
I'd dreamed of planting.
And I know
it will be filled
with blossoms.

And I think, in the dream,
that if I'd seen the door,
if I'd found the room before,
I might have stayed. ¬

SUNDAY MORNING

A storm,
the steady rumble
of a distant ship

draws ever closer,
looms.

I put the kettle on
for tea

lift the honey,
jar of sunlight,
from the shelf.

I rearrange the lilacs
in a yellow vase

set the vase
upon the lace
that drapes the table.

As a child
in the cathedral
Sunday mornings

turning with awe
the gilded pages
of the book

pages as fragile
and translucent
as an insect's wings

my small hands,
brimmed with prayers

prayers, fragile
and translucent

I loved, best of all,
not the high holy days

the weeks of Advent
or of Easter

but those of Ordinary Time.

The sky cracks open,
and the kettle sings.

Incense of rain
and lilacs
fills the air. ¬

Deborah Gordon Cooper

FOUND, LATE APRIL

Between the scattered
scraps of snow

the vestiges of leaves,
first peek of crocuses

a broken rosary

the rift,
between a decade
of Hail Marys

and a final Glory Be

stopping the girl riding by
on her blue-flyer bike
for the first time that year

a wisp of a girl
with tangles in her hair

the girl who quickly
slips the prayer beads
in her pocket.

Later, she will sneak them
in the wooden box
she keeps beneath her bed.

She chooses just one thing
each night

to hold
for dreaming. ¬

SHADOWS

A child might catch,
however briefly

a parent's secret face,
unmasked, alone, afraid

the child, instantly unmoored;
an astronaut, untethered,
grasping

cajoling, with a frantic edge,
the parent back
from that unknown precipice

a quick ruffling of hair,
then walking, hands clasped

to the kitchen
for an ordinary lunch,
cheese toast, sweet oranges

the fleeting terror, passed,
but saved

tucked in that tiny drawer
behind the ribs,
a silent prayer of vigilance.

My father's eyes,
a quiet blue

color of solace,
tranquil waters.

One day,
before he caught me
at the study door

I saw,
beneath the surface
of those waters,
a shadow, floating

before he caught me,
watchful, at the study door

a shape
under the surface
of those waters

something floating,
something drowned. ¬

Deborah Gordon Cooper

Box of Wonders

In the wooden box
beneath her bed . . .

the skeleton key
she'd uncovered
raking leaves

the milkweed pod,
a cradle for a rosary

a ragged stone
with an agate
tucked inside

a tiny statue
of St. Theresa,
glowing in the dark

the wing of a bird,
as blue-black
as the night,
a dream of flight
in every feather

a scapular,
a prayer to wear
against her skin

the fragile bones
of some small
fallen creature,

a chipmunk
or a field mouse
or a wren

a single cufflink
of her Granddad's,
stolen when he died

inside a pearly shell
curled like an ear,
keeper of secrets. ¬

Deborah Gordon Cooper

IF I COULD TAKE BACK

If I could take back
every snide remark

the ways I terrorized
my brothers

and the secret
that I didn't keep

the face I made
in seventh grade

behind the teacher's back,
for all the class to see

Sister Zachary,
but still

the time I mimicked
Chuckie's lisp
out on the playground

and he heard me
and he cried

(later I gave him half my Almond Joy,
but still)

the way I shattered Louie's heart
at seventeen

without a qualm,
without an Almond Joy

moved on to Mike,
who was a drummer in a band,
but still

the one illicit kiss
behind the kitchen door

a kiss that made me
wish for more

the way that I'd replay
the memory . . .
oh, here I go again

the awful day
I snapped at mother

all the times
I lost my patience
with the kids

and you

every time
that I was stingy
with my love

every huff
and every tirade

every time
I turned away

if I could take it back. ¬

CONFESSIONAL POEM

I hid your cake . . .

the chocolate cake
I made from scratch
to show my love for you

the chocolate cake
you had already
eaten half of.

It was something you said,
something significant
and cruel

though it escapes me now.

I watched, last night,
as your eyes scanned
the kitchen
for its whereabouts

though you, wisely,
never asked.

Perhaps you thought
that I had eaten it,
or worse yet,
tossed it in the trash.

Oh, the trash . . .

Deborah Gordon Cooper

Remember your hat?

The brown Stetson
with the hole
in the brim?

The hat you thought you looked
so handsome in?

The one you thought you must've
left somewhere?

The hat with the hole
was fine when we lived
on the farm

not quite fit
for the city though.

Oh, the farm . . .

Did you really think,
when the water
in the middle
of your shower

suddenly blasted cold

on the odd mornings
I was mad at you . . .

did you really think
it was a problem
with the plumbing?

Please forgive me
every bit of it.

Oh, and I hope it helps to know

your cake is safe,
on top of the refrigerator

behind the row of vases,
that were never there before.

Oh, remember the vase?

The crystal one
that had belonged
to your mother? ¬

Deborah Gordon Cooper

ABSOLUTION

Harsh words
this morning.

Now I watch you
from the window

burning fallen branches
in the yard

lost in the flames,
your thoughts

waves breaking
on the shore.

Something goes out of me
to you

and, as if I'd tapped you
on the shoulder

as if I'd whispered
softly in your ear

you turn your face to me
and smile. ¬

TWO REASONS WE ARE LUCKY

(1)

Reading in the evening
we see the moon

lifting from the lake,
dripping light upon the water.

Chapter by chapter,
inch by inch,
she climbs the sky.

When she glides
above the roof
we go to bed.

(2)

I wake you at the day's
first thought of light

to watch the moon's decline
outside the bedroom window

knowing while we slept
she floated over us.

Finally, she slips
behind the maple trees

moonlight tangled briefly
in their limbs.

And when she disappears,
we rise. ¬

YES

I say yes to you
again.

I chose you then
for the gold
the sun wove
through your beard

the waves of your hair,
falling to your shoulders.

I chose you later
for the quiet way
you walk the world

pointing out the small details
I would've flitted past

the way the right light
blues the feathers
of the crow

illuminates the clouds,
caught in a puddle.

I chose you next
for the questions
in your fingers
on my skin

the shy, lopsided grin
it seemed you'd saved for me;
a dozen meanings
in its sweetness.

Today
I say yes to you
again

as I have
across the landscape
of the years

the fields of everydays,
the pitfalls
and high hilltops.

Sometimes,
in a long winter
or a wilting drought

I'd catch your eye
across the table
or the yard

surprised as yes
bloomed again
within my chest.

I watch you now,
reading in your chair

traces of silver
in your beard
and in your hair.

You lift your eyes,
give me that sweet,
lopsided grin

the one you save
for me alone,
ten thousand meanings there

and I say yes to you
again.

How many blossomings
can one bulb hold,
year after year

unfolded by the fingers
of the rain

and this right light? ¬

Deborah Gordon Cooper

THIS TIME

This time
it is the wind
that wakes me

a wind that seems
to be woven
out of voices

out of voices,
familiar and dear,
long silent

and my heart breaks free

and I am hearing my name,
spoken, sung

and I open my eyes,
half hoping.

Lace curtains,
sifting moonlight
on the bedroom floor

and from somewhere
far away
the chime of bells

the kind of bells
that might call us into prayer,
or out of silence.

By my side,
the steady rhythm
of your breath

and I know, if I turn
you too will turn,
without waking

and I know,
if I lean into you and speak

that you will answer,
without waking

and I know what you will say

and the way our words
will drift into your dreams

as now, without waking,
the warm weight of your hand
finds my hip

and my heart settles,
like a bird from flight

with the words
I might've whispered,
might've heard

here now home. ¬

Deborah Gordon Cooper

Because

Because
October's ending
and November looms

each time
I hear a loon
call in the bay

I think that this
may be the last time.

The last magenta
maple leaves

unlatch
the small machinery

that holds them
to the branch.

I pray we all
might fall
as softly. ⌐

About the Author

Blue Window is Deborah Cooper's sixth volume of poetry, following *Under the Influence of Lilacs* (Clover Valley Press, 2010). Her poems appeared in two collections by her writing group of twenty years, including *Bound Together: Like the Grasses* (Clover Valley Press, 2013), winner of the Northeastern Minnesota Book Award for Poetry. Deborah has co-edited three anthologies of poetry, most recently *Amethyst and Agate* (Holy Cow! Press, 2015).

She and her husband, Joel, a visual artist, often work in tandem and frequently exhibit their shared images. She has also worked collaboratively with musicians, dancers, and community theater groups.

Deborah has conducted writing circles with homeless individuals in her community and has taught poetry classes at the St. Louis County Jail for the last ten years. She was the 2012-2014 Poet Laureate of Duluth, Minnesota.

Clover Valley Press
publishes quality books written by women.

CLOVER
VALLEY
PRESS

For more information about our books, go to
http://clovervalleypress.com

www.ingramcontent.com/pod-product-compliance
Lightning Source LLC
LaVergne TN
LVHW021454080426
835509LV00018B/2279